WHO AM I?

I am scaly and snappy, fierce and strong.
I live in swamps and lakes.

WHO AM I?

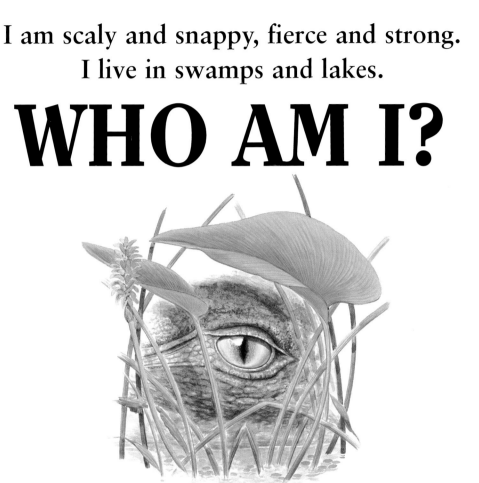

By Moira Butterfield
Illustrated by Wayne Ford

Belitha Press

First published in the UK in 1997 by
Belitha Press Limited, London House,
Great Eastern Wharf, Parkgate Road,
London SW11 4NQ

ISBN 1 85561 598 3 (hardback)
ISBN 1 85561 754 4 (paperback)

British Library in Cataloguing in Publication Data for this book
is available from the British Library.

Printed in Hong Kong

Editor: Stephanie Bellwood
Designer: Helen James
Illustrator: Wayne Ford / Wildlife Art Agency
Consultant: Andrew Branson

My tail is long.
My skin is rough.
It's scaly, thick and very tough.
When my mouth is open wide
you'll see my big sharp teeth inside!

Who am I?

Here is my eye

At night I float in my watery home. My eyes shine in the silver moonlight.

I look for animals to gobble up. If that tasty turtle comes near me I'll pounce on it.

Here is my skin

My skin is very thick to protect me from getting hurt. Look how rough and scaly it is.

When I float in the water I look just like a tree log. Can you spot me in this swamp?

Here is my nose

It is called a snout
and it has two big
nostrils on top.
They close when
I swim under water.

Sometimes I crawl
on to land. I use
my snout to smell
food. This racoon
will be good to eat.

Here is my back

In warm weather
I sunbathe by the
water. I love to feel
the hot sun shining
on my back.

I am long but not
tall. My tummy
drags along the
ground and makes
a muddy trail.

Here is my foot

My feet help me
to swim well. They
have sharp claws.
I use my claws to dig
a den by the water.

Sometimes the
swamp dries out.
I dig a water-filled
hole and stay safe
inside. Who is
sharing my hole?

Here are my teeth

I have 80 sharp
teeth to bite and
tear food. My bite
is so strong that
I can smash a bone.

When I close my
mouth my bottom
teeth are hidden.
That means I'm
not a crocodile.

Here is my tail

I swish my tail and make a loud noise like a lion's roar to tell other animals where I am.

I open my mouth and…
bellow!
Have you guessed who I am?

I am an alligator

Point to my ...

pointed teeth

long tail

sharp claws

yellow eyes

two nostrils

rough skin

I am called an
American alligator.

Here are my babies

They are called hatchlings and they hatch from eggs. I make a cosy nest for them.

The hatchlings are tiny. I have to watch them carefully. Lots of animals would like to eat them.

Here is my home

I live in swamps and lakes.

How many alligators can you count?
Can you find a cottonmouth snake, a bird
called a great white egret and two racoons?

Here is a map of the world

I live in south-east
North America.
Where is it
on the map?

North
America

Can you point to the
place where you live?

Can you answer these questions about me?

How many sharp
teeth do I have?

What is my skin like?

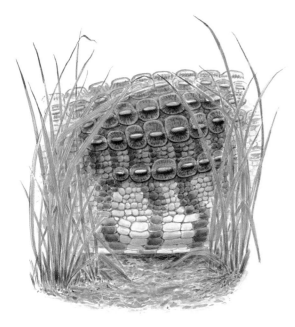

What is my
nose called?

Where do I live?

What are my
babies called?

What colour
are my eyes?

How do I hunt
for my food?

Can you name
some animals
I like to eat?

Here are some words to learn about me

bellow The noise I make. It sounds like a lion roaring. Can you make a bellowing noise like me?

claws My sharp nails. I use them to dig my den in the ground.

den A cosy hole that I dig near the water's edge. I sleep here in winter.

hatchling The name for one of my babies when it has just hatched from its egg.

nostrils The two holes on top of my nose. I breathe through my nostrils just like you.

pounce To jump on something and grab it quickly. I catch my food this way.

scaly Dry and rough. My skin is scaly.

snout My nose. It is wide and it has two nostrils on the top.

swamp My watery muddy home.

trail A muddy path I make when I crawl out of the water on to land.